JUST THINKING

Collection of Poems

———◆———

VOLUME 1

JUST THINKING
Collection of Poems

Volume 1

Abimbola Mosobalaje Davis

Safari Books Ltd
Ibadan

Published by
Safari Books Ltd
Ile Ori Detu
1, Shell Close
Onireke, Ibadan.
Email: safarinigeria@gmail.com
Website: www.safaribooksng.com

In association with:

Books & Sports Limited
15, Mahogany Way,
Forest Hill Estate,
Jericho GRA,
Ibadan, Oyo State.
Website: www.booksandsportsng.com
Email: info@booksandsportsng.com
Tel: +23422913964

ISBN: 978-978-8431-89-3

DEDICATION

To whom my mind gratifies, the custodian of my heart, the love of my love, the peacemaker, Olayinka Motunrayo, thanks for the tolerations. And to those who share from their kitchens to the needy.

CONTENTS

Dedication... *v*

Foreword.. *ix*

Preface .... *xiii*

Acknowledgment... *xix*

Burden 1

Mundane 3

Mama, My Second Soul.. 5

The Kitchen.. 7

Just Sleazy.. 9

The Flood... 11

Shoes... 13

Sorry.. 15

Amazon Maryam.. 17

Cicero... 19

Ode to Death.. 21

Ibadan.. 23

The Teacher.. 25

Covenant.. 27

Codes in the Modes.. 29

Calamity... 31
Song of a Drunkard........................... 33
The Nature....................................... 35
Baami... 37
Chaos... 39
The Capital....................................... 41
Little Trouble.................................... 43
Street Songs..................................... 45
Eso Ikoyi.. 47
Hopeless.. 49
Silk Wood.. 51
Vultures.. 53
Lackluster.. 55
Echoes of Silence............................... 57
The Emperor...................................... 59
Achebe.. 61
Clamour... 63
Ameyo... 65
Ashes... 67
Martha, the Ostrich............................. 69
Education... 71
Kiss has no colour.............................. 73
Exile... 75
Our Faults, my Child........................... 77
Inheritance...................................... 79

FOREWORD

A bimbola Mosobalaje Davis, a professional in business organisational structuring and advisory services, authors *Just Thinking, Vol. I,* a collection of exotic poems, driven by passion and ripples of reaction against failing and failed love, exasperatingly repressive governance, man's inhumanity to nature, and a host of other engaging subject matters. In this collection of poems, the poet explores poetry as catharsis, releasing the locked up emotion of rejection, spewing fumes of revulsion at unreciprocated love and other situations that betray social, economic and democratic ideals.

The poet, fondly called the "Viceroy of Ikoyi Dynasty," brings to bear his high proficiency in the Yoruba language, arts and culture in this collection with his generous use of Yoruba imageries and a rich exploration of the Yoruba history and culture. This is not surprising; Davis is a direct descendant of the Onikoyi, the great warior and protector of the Yoruba race and an avowed advocate of African culture and tradition.

The themes in this vivacious collection include the various sides of love and loving. Betrayed love is presented extensively in "Burden," where he tries to woo his love but "burden's all she brought, leading to the "fears of new beginning incensed (by) the love betrayed." However, reviving and nurturing love leads to the "Covenant" and a mother's undying love in "Mama, My Second Soul," while an unsolicited and calamitous love is depicted in "Just Sleazy," inspired by a fleeting encounter at a train station that looked seemingly inconsequential but must have made an impact. There is also a craving for an ideal reciprocal love that transcends religion, gender, and race as conveyed in "Kiss." Other subject matters engaged by Davis are overwhelming scientific failure, religious catastrophe, natural disasters such as floods and death by fatal diseases, persistent political maneuvering and cataclysm, as well as public officials' corruption.

In addition, Davis explores and commemorates heroism in his celebration of his late father, a review of the prelude to, and the death of the "Cicero", Bola Ige, as well as a florid depiction of Ibadan, the city of his birth, which he holds in great esteem. Other themes include the distortion of historical facts as depicted in Chinua Achebe's last work, *"There was a Country"*, as well as tradition conservation as reflected in the culturally rich *"Baami"* and *"Eso*

Ikoyi," the panegyrics of the "*Agboole Onilu*" of *Itutaba* lineage.

Davis has employed a rich lattice of satire, rhyme, imagery, alliteration and other poetic devices, well conveyed in a colourful vehicle of powerful diction in this collection that is a 'must read' for all across ages, statuses and cultures. I strongly recommend this great work of art for pleasure, didactic and pedagogical purposes.

Adenike Akinjobi (PhD)
Associate Professor of English
University of Ibadan
Nigeria.

PREFACE

Poetry is a work of great artistry which only great minds can discern, the midst of which I like to dwell, conceive and breed, hence this expedition. *Just Thinking* is the considerations and opinions, ideas and judgments, parody, and magnified exposé of observations.

It was a time, when all you dreamt of ended in nightmare and hope bungled in bizarre tension; when you aimed to be a man but ended like a vestal and you gnashed your teeth and paced the forecourt like a vagrant! This aptly described my state of mind when I wrote the "Burden." This happened after my nebulous voyaging in the world of metaphoric instinct, where a man held on to love but ended up in wane; a useful energy dissipated in nostalgic but melancholic affairs. The burden of the spell led to uncertainties and unconsciousness that gave birth to an odious and revolting mind; the outcome of thought, both in agony and harmony.

In the midst of this incursions, my mind was becoming traumatised and was unprepared to accept this unsolicited guest with sharp contrasts, arrived the peacemaker, with whom I later entered into a 'Covenant', a vow of love with a new comer; the Covenant I tenaciously held onto until life itself assures before the emergence of my consummation.

This is the result of my visitations to all strata of the biosphere, and the outcome of my reactions, the good or (if you like) reactionary, to some obstructions caused by human beings!

The deceits by the political leaders, which were captured in the poem, 'Emperor' and their nominated stooges who have brought nothing to the society but tinges of tragedies led to the writing of the 'Little Trouble.' Of course, I believe we are all responsible for their continued imposition.

'Just Thinking – Collection of Poems', brought me into thinking, the thinking that led to several thoughts, and apparently, feud. Yes, feud, an outcome of the clash between my ambitions and her rights! The strife of love by my companion, not to be a widow; or fear of death through killer punch by insomnia!

But in the wake of happiness and new found love came the worst intruder, a flying object or carrier of killer fluid, a case of a preferred death bought from bed-mating, HIV/AIDS, then the unidentified flying object called ebola. I hate the two words, like, *èèdì* and *ẹbo ń lá!* Yes, spell and a big sacrifice!

And before we could complete the procession of the satire, it took our friends, and then we were befuddled by primary school teaching on hygiene, 'wash your hand before you eat," except that this goes beyond that. You are advised to avoid greetings and the devil became venerated and came aboard; then he started making heroes of our being. Though, we sing 'Ode to Death,' we do not want to be dead heroes, yet we celebrate these heroes and heroine! Calamitous death of 'Ameyo' and sadness of losing 'Maryam, the Amazon' to incurable cancer!

The conjecture of my world and the estimation of losses caused through smoking and self-afflictions which were captured in the 'Ashes', an act of ignorance, which sometimes lead to avoidable deaths. In the 'Nature', I spoke against the degradation of soil, the brutality of science in the course of advancing food security, but which has caused reduction in agricultural yields and debilitation and abuse of our environment and natural world.

Then came reasons for friendship, the trust and dilemma of life, who to trust: animal or man? The weaknesses of 'Martha, the Ostrich' brought my trust to Martha, without prejudice to my 'Layinka,' and the bond of love between 'Mama, my Second Soul' and I.

Then, those vitriolic and caustic retaliation or retribution! Or, how can we describe Achebe in

'There was a Country', where he eulogised Biafra, as if, there exists no country before his dream? Hence the poem, 'Achebe', is my reply to his unsavoury diatribe or insalubrious attacks on the Yoruba culture and heroes, especially Chief Obafemi Awolowo.

But casting my mind back at the dialogue between my mother and I regarding my father's warning on 'Inheritance', and the importance of 'Education', one is bound to appreciate the acceptance of guilt by my father and his plea to move on with life. This can also be seen in the poem, 'Not your fault, my Child.'

The greed of our politicians, especially at our former 'Capital', the insatiable greed of the kingpin of our time, the macabre dance of these looters and the erosion of our lives brought about the poem, 'Street Songs.' The poem, 'Lackluster' is about the attitudes of my kinsmen to picking their leaders and the consequences of ignoring the 'Echoes of Silence', à la, uprising, which is dreadfully chilling!

The 'Exile' spoke about the love for the country, loneliness in exile; the fear of the shadow, just because you told the truth and asked for the rights of man and the absurdity of running! Even at that, where I ran to promised no succour, everywhere was laced with landmine!

The solution is in my dream, to see people in the street holding hands and collectively giving a rebirth to this world, when the environment of love assures. Then, my poem, 'Kiss has no Colour', the universality of love and religions, and the need to avoid war will have true meaning.

The dirge for 'Cicero' and the celebration of the 'Silk Wood', my heroes and the time we are in, the exploitation of your minds and mine also informed *'Just Thinking – Collection of Poems.'*

Singing is pleasant to the ears like poetry to the mind, but sound has many colours, styles, tones and meanings. From the local poets to town criers, to composers of good or, if you like, bad songs, who else can do better interpretations or transliterations of the works than the owners? To the great Poet, Alabi Onijala, 'Baami', all 'The Teachers' and those who inspire, here is the usage of the 'words' bestowed on me by you.

Just Thinking – Collection of Poems is a trial for my trial in a field reserved for all but exploited by few. We are all poets, yes, you are.

Abimbola Mosobalaje Davis
2014

ACKNOWLEDGMENTS

I started writing these poems in 2003 when my first marriage ran into a ditch! Although she later came to apologise. She had no tangible reason(s), for her action! That was the period of birth, a foray into literary world when all I cared about was to find a medium to express myself, but as common with many people, it suffered several setbacks. Many factors were responsible for this, principal amongst which are time, personal challenges and dedication. Notwithstanding these events, so many things later shaped and spurred my determination to conclude the book. My wife, Olayinka Apeeti Motunrayo, a great offspring of Odewade, played a major role here. She fuelled my ambition and tolerated my selfishness, the nocturnal voyages to my study, the calls at the dawns to lay within her warmth. She obliged my incessant requests for proofreading during the daytime with encouraging smiles, readiness and reads most times with some delightful, yet dramatic vibrations. She made this book seamlessly possible. 'Whosoever findeth a wife findeth a good thing, and obtaineth favour of the LORD.' She made the true meaning of *Proverbs 18: 22* finally dawn on me. Thank you, Olayinka.

The Safari Books Limited Editorial Team, especially Chief Joop Beckout, Chairman of Safari Books Limited was all I needed to publish my works. The subtle ways he made me do it, the encouragements and confidence he gave became a challenge, which I am happy I took. The words of encouragements of the former Vice Chancellor of Afe Babalola University, Professor Sidi Osho, her sisterly advice and encouragement are invaluable. My editorial team, starting with my wife, as early expressed, my Lawyer, Barrister Tope Adebayo, principal partner at Tope Adebayo LLP and my sister-in-law, Mrs. Oluwakemi Erinle who took her time to look into every word and expression and gave invaluable recommendations and her husband who has always been my 'accomplice' I really appreaciate your contributions. Need I thank my co-voyager, Obalola, Olumide Erinle? I also appreciate Oluwaseyi and Damilola Odewade, for their useful hints on the book.

Our children, Sheriff, the critic, Teniola, Kanyinsola, Olakepemi and Doyinsola were of great support. The two little troublemakers, Jadesola and Obaloluwa were less troublesome during this period.

Adelola Idowu and Bello Adio Numan were always there to share and create fun while Abideen Olugbode suddenly became my pronunciations teacher. Smiles.

I owe many people too numerous to mention so much appreciations. Thank you.

Finally, I thank God for the inspirations and events that trotted my hopes and drove to reality, the dream.

Burden

I have a lot of troubles
My mind is still in rumble
Like a hunter lost in jungle
I tried to find an answer
For the burden I have to shuffle
Frozen, my heart is muffled.

I try to woo my love
That took my love astray
Her voice like Angel beloved
Furnace of love so amorous
Echoes of past enamoured
Burden's all she brought.

Fears of new beginning
Incensed the love betrayed
Antiques of hatred, loss and lust
Hates, sore cremated my heart
Even nature feels the pains,
When we hurt its veins.

---

1   Love betrayed. Written in 2003

Mundane

Life before man made time
Or before time made man

Peace there were for roving souls
Sodom and Gomorrah now baby's roles
Eyes of the Lord now science mole
Bring the moon or clone Dolly
Discoveries of time brought sorry
If not Al Qaeda they are together
Why is man always in misdemeanour
Retaliation rather than integration

He got fret at Babylonians
Where about are His Zionists
Awe! His patience with these unionists
Science has failed in re-union
Rather, it's going for His Kingdom

Occupation but not cooperation
Pollution to control population
Immigration to control inflation
Prophets in colour circulation
Signs of the final cancellation.

---

2   About cataclysms around the world and the failures of science to resolve
     religious crises.

Mama, My Second Soul

From her comes the spring of life
Bearer of ancestral water
Governess of ancient orders
First above the teachers

Aura with different colours
While I call you my 'Second Soul'
He calls you a 'Better Half'
Mama, the ancestral myth

Great descendant of Nature
How much you've suffered
to get me the best in offers
Mama, the crest of my apex

Gladdens heart of discovery
that nothing on earth is kinder
That gives life like mothers
Truly, you are my Second Soul.

---

3   Written in honour of my mother and all mothers.

The Kitchen

He sits alone with awe
Like a man lost his jaws
After efforts run in brawl
What could be his reasons
For running out of season?

He sits among his friends
Like a man who caged his fiends
Everyday he jollies
What could be his reasons
For building such a kitchen?

I found myself in puzzle
Like a kitten wrest in water
Greed all he knows
Care could change the world
If he knows the needy.

A little for the soul
Who sits alone perpetual
With little and nothing to hope
He needs a friend like you
Who owns so large a kitchen.

---

4   This is a story of the poor and the rich and the need to give.

Just Sleazy

My life and lady of lipstick
Disdain for my joystick

Her look reminds of a virgin
Who claimed to be an engine
Every of her clothes were kinky
Confused if she is a junky

Man needs a rest from a beauty
That makes my thinking blurry
Like a lion waiting, pacing
Sitting next to a beauty

The crave of a beauty
But no daddy without a candy
Candy and some goodies
Unless you are grandie

You are just a randy dandy
Without a little candy
Not a stud with lots of spaces
But a dandy with some graces

All she need is my maces
The pleasure of my races.

---

5   Inspired by an incident inside Victoria Train Station in London. The immorality
    of mind.

The Flood

The forest feels the mood
Contest between time and season
Seedlings, farmers musing
Reaping, reason and the season
When sky dances in its nudity

Ostentation of our generation
Anomalous of our arrogation
The abrogation of ancient tether
Like the ellipsis of eclipse
Brawls, between man and nature

Woe betides this deaf duck
Result of man, who denies
Heavenly friend to doss and hops
Gamut of its spectrum
When channels of rains distorted
Market of kings is pallid.

---

6   The 2010 flood that killed residents and disrupted activities in Ibadan, my city.

Shoes

Queuing for my favour
Your promise of a flavour
The past he told like a sailor
Story of his childhood
The growth of his manhood
Life amongst the brotherhood
Where shoes were like diamond
Like a dinner without an almond
Now you, our bailor
Strange admirers of your valour
A click on the google
Without a little struggle
Now a man with muscle
Lo, the promise of the flavour.

---

7   Political sentimentalism.

Sorry

Behold, New Nigeria
And the worries in her Leadership
Where goeth the Sun
That maketh our thinking Independent
The Enquirer will lose his Compass
That giveth the Nation its Guardian
If Vanguard loses its Daily Trust
To the Punch delivered by The News
Lo, the Ovation from the Observer
Oh, Champion of Thisday
Why hath thou forsaken thy Next
So sharp you ruffled the Sketch
In the City of Tribune
Methinks, it's about the City People
Slippery, the mighty are falling
But who will Tell the Channels
Alaroye, or the Parrot?

---

8 Using newspapers and magazines in Nigeria to depict the defeats of the citizens
   by politicians.

Amazon Maryam

Like a bolt off the wheel
A star lost its twinkles
Amazon has finally grown her wings
Dimmed, Sorceress with dimpled nipples
Your absence has brought some ripples

The red has brought its purples
Like a pipe lost its coupler
Mind of men sorrow beset
Phenomenal of your loss
Befuddled stars are since beckoning

Where findeth thy glamour
That shineth like armour
And your smiles that sparkles
Like conflagration with spectrum of colours
The beauty we mourn

Flummoxed, nonplussed and stumped
Your absence has taken grace of death
As confounded women wail
Where goeth Maryam the Amazon
We ponder with hands on chins!

9   Dirge in honour of Mrs. Maryam Babangida, late wife of Nigeria former Military
    President, General Ibrahim Badamosi Babangida, who died of cancer.

Cicero

The word has come home to roost
Ajantala has toppled cap off a Cicero
The man we call our hero
Not by the gods of the Source
But the greed for the purse.

A o m'erin joba
Ewekun ewele

Politics or malady of his ruck
In the city where Oluaye rocks
And the strangers from Sicily
Red their eyes like the chili
Who will tame their gaga?

A o m'erin joba
Ewekun ewele

In a little sleepy hamlet
Where goddess once gave some pampers
Success now laced in angers
Inheritance from the City of Power
But, what makes the Union unbothered?

A o m'erin joba
Ewekun ewele

When our Cicero was altered
Like yam in a mortar
Now mandate of yours he stutters
His dream to inner altar
Run, before your life is altered.

A o m'erin joba
Ewekun ewele

---

10 Dirge in honour of late Chief Bola Ige, former Governor of Oyo State, Nigeria, who was humiliated in the palace of the Ooni of Ife before he was finally assassinated in his residence at Ibadan.

Ode to Death

Cyclone, tornado and whirlwind
Mystery of our wild world
Myth you are in my heart
The death of the purveyor

Growing up with him is an ardour
Custodian of our culture
The denials of the folklores
The scratching of his back.

Whose turn your cudgel will mow?
Skin of which you'll waste
Skilled hunter devoured
Brave I thought was immortal

The sonority in his voice
Ijala that his mates mimic
Even his games revoked
How groans turn to nightmare

Really what is your gain
Oh, cheap hunter of man?
Your games termites eat
How weak you are in skill!

Your credo and the mace
Like Senators hail their phrase
True, we have married our sorrow
With love and flavoured sorrow.

---

11 Celebrating my father in death.

Ibadan

Pepper Clark called you rustic
My mother called you mystic
To me you remain a mystery
The squat hills of Asabari,
That standeth warriors in the face.

Here Kongi held a station
Like a colossus you towered,
Not because you own first towers,
The first viewing station
Or the first listening station;
That you gave the silent nation.

The floss of the savannah
The slush of your sands
The street tirades of Okebadan
Every man with his flaws;
Street fighting is yours, Ibadan.

Innate motherly nature
And your friendly candour
But friends you sent to war!

Yet, you bequeathed some freedom
To siblings with hope for no kingdom
Fights with the feudal lords
Who craved your harbours
Nimble fights of your warriors.

Truly I am proud,
I was born by Ibadan,
The land of great warriors.

---

12 Written to celebrate my birthplace, Ibadan, the most populous city in Africa.

The Teacher

But on our earth you work
Why will heaven pay your wages
His allowance he picks with plea
The rewards of his labour
Those he tended to be sailors
The people he taught, his jailors
His mind now you jailed, you callous!
You captains of his Nation
The man in my foundation
Why are they in his detestation?
Of the man at the lectern
Even bees love their apiaries
Like ants and its colonies
He taught to be caring
On the road to your inventions
Not constriction of your intention
Let earth honours with benediction
And heaven, the grace of his pension
The man at the lectern.

---

13 In support of Academic Staff Union of Universities (ASUU) strike of 2013.

Covenant

Season of love tingles
Let's jolly, sing and merry
The past has gone in oblivion
Ashes of past rekindled
Inconsistencies in unconsciousness
Or a reward for taunting voyagers
And the arrival of a peacemaker
Princess and beauty of my heart
Pacing in the city of penkelemesi
Today the joy has just begun
Covenant of life I made
As love pierced my weakness
Seductive twist in a labyrinth
Peeps, glints, and my friends
The encroachment of gustoes
Oh beauty of my heart, 'Layinka
Remembering pains of the past
To avoid dilemma of the heart
I'll haste to taste in conjugal bliss

---

14 Lover's poem

Codes in the Modes

Stop me not
From using the vessel
For which I was born
This ship from which
I was trained

Stop me not
From riding the horse
For which my ancestral bestowed

Stop me not
From using the words for which I was moulded
As from her womb will
come a thespian

Stop me not
Or leave me be
As my words are exact
Mathematical or scientific
Words which made me an African

---

15 The poem is written in protest against the dearth in African culture, especially in
Nigeria where we are rapidly losing our mother tongues to English language and
foreign civilisation.

Calamity

If I were to be the son of a king
I will ride a horse to pluck some leaves
For the sons of kings kill with levity.
If I were to be the son of a chief
I will sit on man and ride on women
The son of chief rapes and cages
Happy I am I was born of a sage
Morals he taught me with gauge
Humble he lacks the son of the king
Gather rather from the meek, they sing
Until the beginning of the stinks
When calamity befell the sons of our kings.

16 About a former Governor in South West Nigeria and his spoilt children.

Song of a Drunkard

Oh spirit of my destiny
Where goeth thy visions
Years before the arrival of the gullible
Oh democracy! Arrant did mumble
Worshippers we were to the uniform
Before godfathers swapped the academy
Contests of men and their rustic peers
Men lay in means rather than ends
Politicians and their macabre dance
Prosperity kept us in trance
Vote for me, is oats for you
Now clergies, the czars of our minds
Prequel to the brotherhood
Apostates, or descendants of Christ
And the fanatics of His Rival
My redemption has since forsaken
Moral decline brought by conspiracy of elders
How many generations you maimed
Siblings all in emotive wane
Spirit of my destiny

---

17 This is about religious fights, the political upheavals in Nigeria, stealing with
impunity and tortures to the minds of the citizens.

The Nature

Here is where it began
Where man reneged on the oath
Believeth she of man
Partner in the covenant
Vows she held so tight
But loose the descendants of man
Like a child and his umbilical cord
Some you made royal
Not because they play loyal
Artists and their mimicry
Depleted and unhappy, she cries
While he called it excavation
Hurt, because of this demarcation
'Oh, my veins you tore!
Pains, sore, are my mammary!
Arteries wounded and seizure
Acclamation of my soil,
Depleting of my trees
But amongst you stands a Saviour
To stop the fury of your nature
Please stop earth degradation.

---

18 A cry in support of organic agriculture and aforestation.

Baami

Where goes Alabi Eso?
By whose mouth I weaned
Chanting of Ijala ode and oriki orile
Alujonjonkijon and other folklore
Your tale of the dove
That he held so tight
The death of Onirese
And the breaking of his carves
The proverbs of Jontolo
Your narrative of the sleeping Chiefs
Ohun to ba'ni laa ran
My journey to storytelling
Your early morning rites
Supplication to ogun
May Ogun protect us all
Milieu of my culture
And the arrival of the caveat
Circumspection to my tradition
Your departure to the procession
Lost inclination to my tradition.

---

19 Warning on the decline of our culture.
    *Baami – My father

Chaos

Back to my village
Scattered were my haulage
Hopes great they were
Dreams of these young men
Caught in era between two laws
Like wars win with wails
Government becalmed and stagnant
Internal upheavals, political horrors
Scarred by hostilities, losses unimaginable
Futures mutilated, bodies unidentifiable
Violent ideologies of our 'Saints'
Politics of disdains, ignorance of the past
Oh you bloodlust!
Barbarous deaths like holocaust
Come here for justice
A kiss on the guillotine

---

20 Economic instability and political violence.

The Capital

When you get to Lagos
Remember your Creator
Before you put up with Abby
In a city with lullaby
Long before my cohorts
But the arrival of my ancestors
Histories of honours belittled
When they tarnished my culture
Enslavement of men with valour
Not without some ruptures
Years of great mediators
Booming the capital has become
Influx of foreign chicanery
Religious bigotry in municipalities
Cultures dilapidated but assimilated
Capitulation of capital in the Capital.

---

21 Doing comparisons, between the past and the present, talking about the dwindling
economy of Nigeria.

Little Trouble

This our little pass; jazz for your further cadge
Roaming for its prey, setting us a bait
Even when bewildered; we reasoned not to be withered
Why the little trouble; and his double troubles
Trust stucked in rubbles; like grumble for the rumbled
No choir for the jumble; like the heaps for the muddled
Mockery of his godfather, his heritage that he sunders
In the days of his pleadings: begging, he begins to mutter
Hope of a station, to bring more inventions
State and lost intentions, markets lost in tensions
When mouth has no meaning; musing could be dizzying
Reserves of our labour; proceeds of his tricks
The hopes in our ballots; the frizzled of the harlots
Who will help our sorrows or bellow for our tomorrow.

---

22 Politicians, the tricks and the sorrow they brought.

Street Songs

Remembering my days with buccaneer
Not like dingy of abracadabra
Hopeful of life we bubbled
But advent of the shakabulas
Street songs are now halleluias
Dane guns, double barrels and AK47
Run for cover or reign in heaven
Streets songs are now Armageddon
Neighbours suspicious of the kingdom
Doors of hatred magnified
They hail democratic dictator
Alas, his party like robot
Not yet in mood for the dirge
Just marvelled at this dredge
Societal misplaced opportunist
Sorry, Lagos for your misfortunes.

---

23 Greed of a man who wants to own all Lagos properties and Southwestern
   Nigeria, his insatiable appetite for power and fleecing of States' resources through
   his cronies.

Eso Ikoyi

Onikoyi, the great warrior
Protector of my clan
Progenitor of my source
Your basket flows with mischief
Who else parks his oodles
In expectation of his death
But you, Yanbimlolu
Date of your death you heard
But drums you trundled
Death threats you issued
To the court of the king
My tribe and its substance
Bravery, my birthright
War, my heirloom
But fear is me, the Duke
Viceroy of your ancestors
To carry your mettle
Imperial Majesty of Ikoyi Dynasty
To take arrows in my torso
The rite of your forebears

---

24 Panegyrics of my ancestral clan, Eso Ikoyi.

Hopeless

Hopeful for today
Troubles like folkloric turtle
Ambition of man to rule
Like the love that is alien
Aspiration to govern a Nation
He calls himself the Leader
Craziness begets a Section
To light the nation with a lantern
Barbarous investment in the Nation
Tribulation is the notion
But we are not your turkey
Failed, your ideas on turnkeys
Oh you refined junky
Enemy of my Hero
Curse for you tomorrow
Hopeless you are to my Region.

---

25 Found myself in a situation where I had to reply to a political kingpin who was using his newspapers to attack the family of the late Yoruba hero, Chief Obafemi Awolowo.

Silk Wood

Oh man with silver hair
The man with bronze skin
Sneers, scorns, gibes and taunts
Politically motivated persuasions
Nay, generation yet not wasted

Oh man with silver beards
Need I rely on the seers?
Without your pranks we tear
Tall you are like a silk tree
I remember the mask of yours

Occupation of a station
Albeit your vision of a nation
Jaw-dropped were your peers
Onset of brother Jeros
Incursion, or, the man died

To the beckoning of Wild Christian
From Ake womb you came,
Ecclesiastic traditionalist,
Our palmwine Captain
Meritorious atheist
or elusive Chaplain

---

26 Written in honour of Noble Laureate, Professor Wole Soyinka.

Vultures

They wouldn't allow me to further
Because my words is not formal
We refused the order
They ordered us not to bother.

In the city of the Adventists
And the selling of their cultures
My ancestors were in ventures,
Before the ventures of the vendors

Hazard bemoaned our medics
Acceptance of their relics,
Before you share their ration
You must be in their action.

Not hailing their tradition
Is like ignoring their fashion
Like a future in ruckus,
Mistakes are these vultures.

27 Talking about religious bigotry and public officials corruption.

Lackluster

Our guy they called indolent
Some called him impotent
A paralytic paraphrase
Like a casual filthy craze
As sunrise awaits a farmer
Rather than waiting for the rain
Kolo mental or mental in the colony
Another arrival of the madman
When a man wears leg chains
A woman you are or man in derision?
But he was once a Governor
Or maybe a lost honour
Metaphysical power against legal jingoism
Like putting salt in a honey
Acrobatic dance by the cripple.

---

28 Personality questions! The Governor and his skin bleaching.

Echoes in Silence

This silent noise
This peeling voice
The rudderless cows
When goats like cat mows
Oh doomed we are
Friends and junked stars
Honour yet misplaced
The pillagers of our age
Demagogue they bloomed
Sprouting of the doomed
He called it generation wasted
Or an era burdened
Whilst skies cry and refuse blues
These silent footsteps
As Nation move towards mayhem
Alas! our generation next
Oh, echoes of silence.

---

29 The looming revolution.

The Emperor

Here comes Billingsgate
Emperor and his ballooned age
Smiles amongst the egoists
The people he mimics
Comics and their bowler hats
And his perpetual wrapper
Why gnashing of our teeth
Losses caused by his perfidious aides
Greed and the successor's raids
Misuse of our ancestral inheritance
The waste of his anointed Prince
Oh God safe our souls
And the beleaguered kinsmen
The careworn multiple poor
Emperor alluded to the sored King
But I've seen why he cringed.

30 The brawls between two Presidents, one still serving and a former.

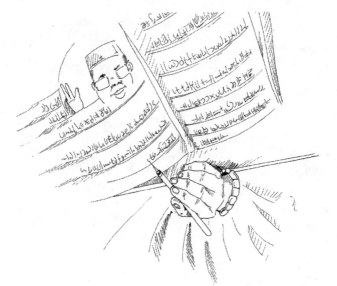

Achebe

Night before the dawn
Hero of ours you yawned
Before these satirical nuances
Unlike Okonkwo and Ikemefuna
Like the innuendoes in new epistle

Now things you fell apart
You Master of diatribes
Truly you lost a country
With your oratorical eloquence
Your visit to Saro in his opulence.

While you dreamt of your country
Before things fell apart
Cruel are you death
Or why his mouth in menopause
Grace you gave the Chief Priest.

Departure of Chief Tribalist
Reactions to his hatred
When he brought down the Centre
The Centre we held dear
The cradle of your Master's ambition

Torrent of blood in the field
Records of past you maimed
Vaccination of your inclinations
Caustic to my tribe you raved
To heroes of my region, you warped
Careful we were before your drool
Peace we thought your name
Until our centre you gook
Truly 'things you fell apart'
Before things fall apart.

---

31 In reply to Chinua Achebe for his attacks on the late sage, Chief Obafemi
Awolowo and the Yorubas, and for twisting the history of Nigeria civil war in his
last book, *There was a Country.'*

Clamour

Hope is all about hope,
when events trots hope
and tilt towards positivity.
When action of man demeans
the essence of hope is lost.
Rise we as arbiters
to fight the wrecks created in hope.
or there will be no hope in hope!

Dreams can only be inspired by vision,
vision by mission, mission with passion,
and passion to drive the mission.

32 A contribution to Harvard Business Review Linkedin page, an online magazine's discussion in 2014.

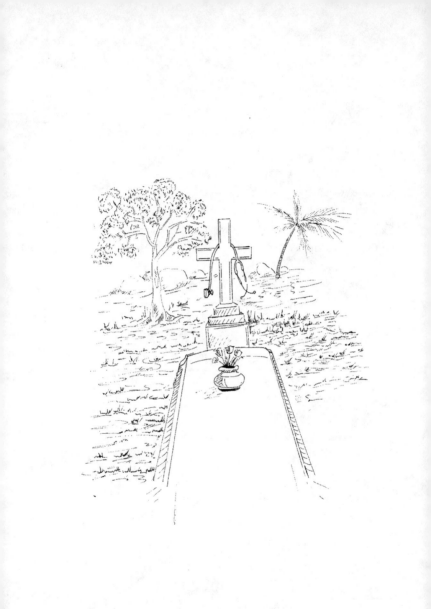

Ameyo

What about the malady
They claimed it's acidic
Before dumping in the ditch
Friends they are in cellophane
In the city with flying beasts

Echoing of lullaby
Dirge and wail for heroine
Milky breasts to a dying friend
But unkind man who took her life
A strange visitor in our midst

The death he brought from beyond
His capricious caprice
Her deign to save his life
Perpetuity with hero's past
Earth petrified, minds aghast

When Sawyer sold sour taste
Ameyo paid in haste
Nay, cold war, world war but big horror
Great clan of our hero
Go ye with honours

---

33 Dirge in honour of Dr. Stella Ameyo Adadevoh who lost her life to ebola while
trying to save Mr. Patrick Sawyer, the first person to bring ebola to Nigeria.

Ashes

In the midst of the converts
All they wear is cravats
Not about the graveyard
Freedom of my action

The right to self-cancellation
Or cancellation of addictions
Craving of infatuation
A ban on my decision

Ashes is your soul, I reject
Warm is my heart, I inject
Mailing of the inhale
Like dying and the wail

Excuses for my habits
Result of the tidbits
Cancer for the maddened
When a smoker is hardened.

---

34 About the danger in smoking.

Martha, the Ostrich

Her neck like a tether
Reminding me of Cleopatra
Queen of heart and clime
Roses of her neck
Gracefulness of her legs
Dancing in her steps
The beauty of her body
Warmness of her tone
Like Louis and his baritone
Gazing like a sis
Like the sternness of Isis
The pride in your skill
But in cage you are
Doubt man, but not you
My friend, Martha, the ostrich

---

35 Inspired by the beauty of my Ostriches and the trust they display anytime I'm
around them.

Education

I've gone below
I've known 'hello'
The right to know
Is just your role
To get hallowed

The marrow of the tutor
Like the candour of a suitor
Fire in his soul
The hopes in his roles
The fervour for your goals

Reasons for your role
Caution not to wallow
The height of your goal
The focus on your mold
Celebration of your threshold

Dream to be hallowed
Or rejection of your load
The end of your road
Subscription to the dole
When you fail to be hallowed.

---

36 Using this poem to depict the importance of education and hard work.

Kiss has no colour

Differences I knew not
In your kisses and hers
Marylyn and my Maryam
The succulence of your lower lip
And the strength in her upper lip
The feel of your waist
Like a touch on a suede
The tenderness in her touch
And the sleekness of her skin
Like the meekness of a lamb
The sensuous tinge in her gaze
Your kisses and hers
Marylyn and my Maryam
Kiss has no colour
I've seen the warfare
When faith doubts faith
And a case of no fate
Let's drop the waging rage
And marry all faiths
Let's know no colour
But dictation of our aura
Because, kiss has no colour.

---

37 Kiss and love is a universal practice for all genders, race and country. I have
used 'kiss', as a symbol of love. The poem preaches peace and tolerance amongst
Christians and Muslims.

Exile

My sojourn in obscurity
Visions of home I yearned
Running was all I learnt
I know I'm not a bandit
Because I own no armoury
But because I'm out of boundary
They thought I caused their quandary
Caution's just the option
When vestige of hope is lost
Strength to crawl is bust
But in the bosom of a stranger
Providence is all my song
Hopeful for today
Doubtful am I for tomorrow
When will I see my country?

---

38 Encouraged by my wife to write a poem about my fears and loneliness while I was
in exile.

Our Faults, my Child

There is no inheritance, my child
We have wasted the abundance
Not by happenstance
But our lack of resistance

In you resides the substance
The persistence of your perseverance
The awakening of the sleeping being
The giant that dwells in you

The insistence of your rights
The restoration of the honours
The honours that we sundered
The relics to be gathered

Legacy of our misdeeds
The creeds that we falter
Not yours to alter
Move on and be better

---

39 It was a sermonic poem. The idea is to accept the failures of our leaders and
citizens but to encourage the youths, reminding them that their future and that of
the country lays before them.

Inheritance

Words of your father, sayeth mother
Not to rely on his fortunes
His affluence and his riches
Collection in his harems
Denial to live in his opulence
But crave to build your legacy

Sufferings he bestowed on you
To go and plough your farm
Landmine awaits your foot, he said
But treasure sits below
You have to dig the earth
The words that he spewed

His lips you will inherit
Your ways, his deeds to lead
Off the landmine and unto the field
The dignity in your humbleness
A little of what you give
Bequest to your growth

Remembrance of the landmine
Devotion to his cautions
The wisdom of the wise
The saliva of his age
Inheritance that he gave
That, will make you a man

40 Advice to the youth about the challenges ahead of them.

Printed in the United States
By Bookmasters